T0114644

TheThrone of the Ghost

TheThrone of the Ghost
A play

by

Modou Lamin Age-Almusaf Sowe

malthouse 𝄢

Malthouse Press Limited

Lagos, Benin, Ibadan, Jos,Port-Harcourt, Zaria

3

© ModouLaminSowe 2016
First published 2013
New Edition 2016
ISBN: 978-978-949-713-3

Published by
Malthouse Press Limited
43 Onitana Street, Off Stadium Hotel Road,
Surulere, Lagos, Lagos State
E-mail: malthouse_press@yahoo.com
malthouselagos@gmail.com
www.malthouselagos.com
Tel: +234 802 600 3203

*Distributed by the African Books Collective Ltd
Oxford, UK*

Dedication

''Say he is Allah the One;'' Holy Qur'an says in Surah Al-Iklăs, chapter 112, verse 1

'' Say: It has been revealed to me that a company of Jinns listened to the Qur'an. They said, 'We have really heard a wonderful Recital! ''It gives guidance to the Right, and we have believed therein: we shall not join (in worship) any gods with our Lord''. Holy Qur'an says in Surah Al- Jinn, chapter 72, verse 1-2

Acknowledgements

Edited in The Gambia by Lawyer Lamin K. Mboge of Maribantang Chambers Fatoumatta Cassama of Gambia Maritime Administration (GMA); Aunty Ramatoulie Othman of Gambia Maritime Administration (GMA); Abridged and simplified outside the Gambia by Dr. Toby Green, Lecturer in Lusophone African History and Culture, Departments of History and Spanish, Portuguese and Latin American Studies, King's College, London, UK.

I owe my heartfelt appreciation and gratitude to my father, Alh. Gorgy-Ebrima Sowe, mother Aja. Lala-Mariama Saye, my faithful step-mums: Fatou Jammeh, Isatou Njie, Fatou Bah and Ida Sowe; my lovely sisters, Haddy-King Sowe, Fatou Sowe, Hulimatou Sowe, Neneh-Galleh Sowe and all well wishers of our dear country The Gambia.

My appreciation also goes to Mr. Hassoum Ceesay of the National Centre for Arts and Culture (NCAC) for all his support. I thank him for his encouragement and guidance. I wish him and his family all the best.

Preface

This piece of work was originally aimed at enhancing better performance at the West African Senior Secondary School Certificate Examination (WASSCE) for students studying Literature as a subject.

It has in all its explanations sufficient ingredients of Literature and depicts African culture, precisely The Gambia. The play, though aimed at the level of secondary school students, it may also be suitable for some courses at the tertiary level. The language used is simple with a Glossary provided for candidates and readers. The play should equip students with tools of understanding in order to tackle likely examination questions they are expected to answer.

Considering education as the golden cage in which the eggs of success must be laid, I engaged my minor skills in creative writing to provide a nest for all learners of Literature and other research persons.

I must say that utility is satisfaction, but if you do not utilize the resources you have at your disposal, how can you be satisfied? I hope that the Ministry of Basic and Secondary Education (MoBSE), and all Gambians will find my work valuable and, more so, patronize it. A farmer never had any knowledge of how weeds grow in his farm; therefore, let us supply the tools in the hands of the students themselves to weed the national farm in order to know the sweat and pain it takes to be a patriot.

The students of any country are the present and they are the future, and if any society neglects their voice, they shall be left without any future.

Modou Lamin Age-Almusaf Sowe (Sowisticality)
November, 2013

Contents

Dedication
Preface
Characters   11
1. Scene One   12
2. Scene Two   19
3. Scene Three   22
4. Scene Four   25
5. Scene Five   28
6. Scene Six   33
7. Scene Seven   39
8. Scene Eight   43
9. Scene Nine   47
10. Scene Ten   49
11. Scene Eleven   54
12. Scene Twelve   49
13. Scene Thirteen   62
14. Scene Fourteen 66
15. Scene Fifteen   69
16. Scene Sixteen   72
17. Scene Seventeen 75
18. Scene Eighteen 79
19. Scene Nineteen 82
20. Scene Twenty   85
21. Scene Twenty-one 89

22. Scene Twenty-two   91
23. Glossary   96

Characters

King Saliman: The King of Niamina Dankunku
Awa: The first wife of the King
Fatou: The second wife of the King
Ishaq: The eldest son
Sheriff: The second son
Suaib: The slave
Oumie: The eldest daughter and a sister to Sheriff
Astou: The youngest daughter and a sister to Ishaq
Zaib: The eldest man in the Kingdom and Head of
     Council of Elders
Cherno: The Kingdom's Fortune Teller
Gawlo: The Kingdom's Praise Singer
Imam Ratib: The Imam of the Kingdom
Maimuna: The Jinn
Oustas: A Quranic Teacher
Young-Girl: The Sacrifice
Stranger
Great Man: Marabout
Mariama: A Jinn
Jinn

SCENE ONE

SETTING

It was on a Saturday, after a heavy rain which had left the birds shivering with cold, the wind opened its great black wings and flew across the world carrying its army and, as it advanced across the skies, bringing darkness and chaos of lightning with it.

Saliman, the King of Niamina Dankunku, opened his mouth and his bottomless throat and let loose a thunderous roar. The waters flooded the streets to stop the shepherds and hunters from returning home in time and, in the battle beneath the world's roof, the sun, like a red beast, drowned. As the traumatic disease of the King struck him severely, he summoned a meeting quickly in his palace.

King Saliman: I summoned this meeting today
purposely to inform you about a strange
happening that will soon befall my Kingdom—
(He stopped and speaks in proverbs):
As we all know that my kingdom is feared all
over the world, as a result of strong men with
its rich culture, but the big tree firmly holding
these fruits in a garden with only two ripe
fruits on it, is about to lose his roots.

(**Zaib** who understood this proverb quickly bowed
down his head in grief and asks a question)

Zaib: Your Honour, but who is going to water the
garden in the absence of the tree among the
two fruits?

King Saliman: The first one to fall—
(The meeting is suspended for a few minutes
and resumes as the King continues to assure
his people about his predicament.)

King Saliman: I assure you that among my two
wives who are heavily pregnant, anyone of
them who first gives birth to a son shall be the
heir to my throne and must be named Ishaq.

(**Suaib** enters unexpectantly and interrupts the
meeting)

Suaib: Your majesty, Great Cherno is here to see you.

Awa: What is this termite doing in the meeting of lizards?

King Saliman- Close that your wallet you call a mouth before me...Let him come in.

(Cherno starts praising the king as he enters)

Cherno: King Saliman the mightiest, the mahogany tree, for the pen is mightier than the sword, the man of substance, the fire that burns stones, the hole which fills ditches, for the snake has never failed to father long things, the son has come out from his father, the mountain which produced his own water during the dry season, the man with gums that can bite, *''Bah Pullo Jeerri''*.

King Saliman: Thank you, you may be seated.

Fatou: If the cook hates the knife, she will always cry from the bulk of onions she slices.

King Saliman: Enough! Cherno I am sorry that I forgot to send for you, but you even caught up

15

with us at the right time. Can you consult your oracle for my two wives?

Cherno: Yes I will do so, My Honour! *Abracadabra, 'Salalli Muhammad Walla Muhammad, Saakaja Makka Jaa, Ay! Ay! Ay! '* in honour of the sun, by the moon ah! Your Majesty!
The banana tree does not stay by the riverside without bringing forth offsprings...the sun that shines on the shape of the soul to show its soap...the wind which whirls the windmill and weans its wise...the wishes that wash witchcrafts...

King Saliman: Speak.

Cherno: It is the second source of your heart which pleases your septum and not your aorta that is always jealous that you have two kidneys, but the grave opens its heart for the coffin waiting to be opened at the graveyard.

Awa: What do you mean Great Cherno?

Cherno: Those whose eyes can see their ears know what I mean.

Zaib: On the whole, a bitter tomato might be white but the roots dark in colour.

Gawlo: Just as I thought Zaib. Let me tell you how Suaib was made a royal slave. This has to do with history and I am the only resource person to narrate our rich and beautiful culture to the young ones. His father was a renowned debtor and couldn't pay his debts to Our Majesty. As a result, he had to compensate the King with his one and only adored son. Suaib came to this palace when he was only seven years, and considered as the favourite slave to King Saliman amongst all the royal slaves.

Zaib: This reminds me so much of the battle we fought gallantly, in which I made so many men grovel on their knees in honour of my sword.

King Saliman: Suaib!

Suaib: Yes, My Honour.

King Saliman: Serve them some milk and food. It is almost daybreak and very soon you will all begin to see your footsteps. Culture is a virtue which should be championed by every society in the twenty-first century, including the future generations yet unborn, but it can't be socially harvested without being morally implanted into the womb of our environment which, directly or indirectly, transmogrifies the human psyche.

17

My final word is that you must all unite, especially my wives.

(They leave the Palace and light converted and picks Oumie, from where she has been standing.)

SCENE TWO

It is morning at the King's Palace, Oumie woke up feeling dizzy and unhappy.

* * * *

OUMIE: Aaahhh! Today my limbs are motionless because I have not eaten. No. Maybe I lost my way. Could this be a mere dream? I saw myself happily laughing in a dream.

(She is interrupted by a loud cry: "Oh He Died, His Majestic is gone." The lamentation continues from a nearby distance. They all rush out to pin-point the scene, as the news spreads like melted limbs of a cow; Zaib enters the house where the body is laid.)

Zaib: For it is said that you don't know what you have till it's gone; God gives and takes lives anytime He wishes. You can't love a person more than God; death was created first before life. Death is the only price every soul must pay for. You nearly put me in tears when my conscience as a man inhibited the flow of my tears from the stream of my eyes.

We will all die one day. Calm down my dear women, for lamentation shall not raise the dead but only disturbs them. The Qur'an says ''every soul that taste life must taste death''. Here lay a man of God, a prominent 'Hafis'; a man whose right hand gives more than he earns; he whose orders always dictate the sunnahs of the Holy Prophet Muhammad (S.A.W), and the teaching of the Holy Qur'an. The kingdom of Dankunku has indeed lost a great man, but let us not forget that when you lose a golden ear-ring, your ears will always take the same size of ear-ring it is used to. All of you here, I implore you with honesty and truth, to come forward and tell us if he owes anyone of you and we shall settle the debt on his behalf before he is finally laid to rest.

(Silence reigned for a moment...few minutes later)

Imam Ratib: 'Alhamdoulilah', we thank God that he didn't die owing anyone, I now demand that we offer him our last prayers before carrying him to the graveyard.

(His words seem to be a relief to the natives and family of the deceased, as the women drown in their tears, regrettably weeping farewell tears to the king. Consequently the burial is done and they pray for him)

(*Suaib enters, soliloquizing*)

SCENE THREE

It is two weeks after the death of the King; Suaib the royal slave appears at the palace and thinks in (Utopia). He talks to himself undesirable without any listener.

Suaib: Oh death, the separator of the dear from the dearest, is a person strong enough against you?
If not for your bravery, His Majesty wouldn't have died. I wish I can raise him from his grave and give him life.

(Zaib interrupts him)

Zaib: Only God can do that. Prepare the horse-cart to ride our queens to "Wuli".

Suaib: ''Cow''? Hope you are not making a mistake? Wuli means hotness in "Fulani' language.

Zaib: Let me broaden your horizon. Some words might sound exactly the same in English, but completely different in meaning and spelling.

The word ''Cow'' means "an uncle" in Fulani language. Such words are known as homophones, I was lucky to be taught this from a close friend of King Saliman during our encounter with the French after the Anglo-French trade rivalry. I was going to teach you more before I left. Nimble-footed, you haphazardly educated lad, celebrated fool!

Suaib runs faster than his eyes can see, adhering to the order given to him.

Light takes Fatou, Gawlo and Zaib sitting in the living-room at the king's palace.

SCENE FOUR

In the house of Fatou the second wife of the late king. She is having a discussion with Gawlo and Zaib.

Fatou: Ooohhh! This is indeed a blessing! I gave birth first, and I am so delighted it's a son.

Zaib: Thank Allah for his blessings; this rain has flooded hearts with a bitter-sweet joy.

Gawlo: Meaning he will be the heir to the throne.

Fatou: Yes I hope so.

(Suaib enters the house)

Suaib: Have you heard the news?

Astou: Which news is that again? Who died?

Suaib: No one died. It is just that Awa also gave birth to a son.

Gawlo: What a success is in this consecrated family?

26

Fatou: I only wish my dear husband was alive to see for himself the seeds he has sown.

Gawlo: Calm down Fatou! Don't source the rivulet of the eye which is almost dry for now. Please Suaib, make sure that the news is spread well as in accordance with our tradition. Since today is Friday, it means next week Friday shall be the naming ceremony. Do you hear me?

Zaib: No!!! Don't even trouble him into that. I will make it my duty. But let us remember that we were reliably informed by His Majesty that the first son should be the heir to the throne and must be named Ishaq.

Fatou: *Cow*! We can all recall that. We all have to know that the seeds of culture are always implanted into the womb of our environment. Let's just stick to our tradition because you know that our culture is what was left here for us by our forefathers.

SCENE FIVE

The following week Friday, it is the naming ceremony at the king's palace, everyone is flamboyantly dressed.

Zaib: Our Queens, please bring our sons for the naming.

Imam Ratib: Let us join our hands and pray for the prosperity of our sons, and also for the departed soul of their late father to rest in perfect peace, *Bismillah*!

(After the naming)

Zaib: In our tradition, when a child is born, we normally name him the following week on the same day that he was born. What we will even do in our culture is to name that child after someone we value, so that child from infancy is being given a role-model. The Western societies have not risen to that level, and even if they have, it must have been in the past.

Imam Ratib: The Holy Quran has also stipulated the Rights of a Child and the responsibilities of their parents towards their nurturing.

Stranger: *Mi sallmi nii oon bandirabeh!* Ya-Imam, this point is seriously misunderstood today by our people in Africa. It is a thing we talk so much about, Child's Right, rights all the time! Nevertheless, I want us to know that every right goes with a responsibility. As a result, if we are to go back to the 13th and 14th centuries, we would realize that the world had gone through a process of fighting against colonial domination, industrialization, and people kept on fighting against monarchies, liberating countries, until they came to realize that we must create a suitable environment. It all started in the form of an idea from one person, then it developed into two, to three and graduated to a clan, to a region and then to a country and finally to the world. So what we are saying is the right of the child is actually the responsibility of its parents.

Crowd: *Hmmm!*

Zaib: Young man, thank you so much for making us clearly understand this point. What we thought as Africans is that Child's Right has come to pamper our children and thereby make them indisciplined and casual towards their elders.

Stranger: That is not Child's Right; the right of a child as enshrined in both the Constitution of the Gambia, the Children's Act of 2005, including the United Nations Convention on the Rights of a Child (UNCRC), have all talked about the inalienable rights of children. In their entire article, you will not find a single critic, which guaranteed young people the right to disobey their elders. For instance, a child has the right to go to school, but it is the responsibility of the parents to take him to school. Our elders thought that this is a Western Ideology, but, to be frank, this has existed even before the Europeans strayed along the Atlantic Coast.

Zaib: Thank you so much, my son, and I hope that everyone here will make the best use of your points and henceforth utilize them. My son, before we disperse, I will like you and everyone here to pay attention to how culture and environment can influence one's life. These influences are in two, namely Environmental Influence of a society which adopts an existing concept as a social value; a perfect example of this is the Mandingo ethnic group as the

31

dominant tribe in The Gambia. In most cases, culture is seen as an object of civilization over a long period of time by the same ethnic-group, sex, family or surrounding. Here, an idea from one person or a group influences the same people in a particular surrounding sharing the same historical background.

Crowd: *Hmm*, we never knew.

Zaib: Secondly, when people evolve, this happens as a result of a mixture of cultural values and environmental adoption; cultural Influence happens as a result of an ancestral belief or practice of an individual or a group which is handed down from one generation to another. An example of such could be the Fulas, Serehules, Wollofs, *et cetera*. Culture and environment are used as agents to influence others through practices and beliefs.

Stranger: These have answered my question and will help me in my research on how culture and environment can influence one's life. Thank you *Cow*, for what an elder sees, even if a child stands on the skies he won't see it.

SCENE SIX

(EIGHTEEN YEARS LATER)

It is a day for Qur'anic recitation amongst children in the entire realm at the king's palace; everyone is in traditional attires.

Imam Ratib: All praises be to Allah, the Lord of the Universe! Today marks yet another day for national reflection, as it was organized by His Majesty who was a proud sponsor of this annual event. This occasion is to articulate and re-emphasize the concept of Islamic principles and practices in our vicinity. The event is quite different from the previous because today our main concern shall be which child can properly recite the Holy Qur'an by heart. As the Head of the Committee, I now declare the event open!

(The children formed a queue to recite the Holy Qur'an from "Bakara" to "Naas", till there came in the two sons of the late king as finalists).

Sheriff: *''Allahu laahilaha-illahuwa''*—

(He stammered and could not complete the ''Ayah'').

Then came in the eldest son of the late king, Ishaq, who smoothly recited it all by heart.

Zaib: It is not a competition, but it's to let young people know about their Lord and Religion.

(Light picks Maimuna and her friend, Mariama, having a discussion at the back of the audience unseen by the people.)

Mariama: Maimuna, you have been concentrating too much and have completely glued your eyes on that lad. I only hope that you are not being attracted to him?

Maimuna: As if you've read my mind! I have been following him now for eighteen years and would make him dream about me. We were born on the same day, but he is not an ordinary human being. He is so multi-talented and could be something for Africa in years to come. I am always jealous anytime he talks to other women, and I have to make him sick. But anytime he sits alone, I will join him unseen and stop all what I may be doing because I love

35

watching him smile. As we are sitting in the midst of this audience, I am still wondering whether we Jinns can marry human beings! My love grew deeper for Ishaq having heard him recite the Holy Qur'an. In Africa, leaders are not just mere people, but indeed people with foresight. At the end of the Qur'anic recitation, I will like to talk to him.

Mariama: Wowwww! You are madly in love with him I see! Honestly, he is a perfect gentleman with unpretentious manners; he is so kind, caring, clean, pious, intelligent and down to earth. Adding to his generosity with his money, these made him unavoidable priceless to women. I don't know whether he has magic or what!

Maimuna: That's him over there. Let me summon my courage and talk to him.

(She calls Ishaq to an isolated place.)

Maimuna: My dear—I *hmm*— sorry— I call you to this isolated place to know more about you. Can you spare me a minute please, and let me talk to you?

Ishaq: No problem. I only hope it's not going to take long.

Maimuna: Well—just as I wish. God has many things in store for you if only you will listen to me.

Ishaq: Allah burdens not any soul beyond its capacity. Whatever you are about to ask me to do, just consider it done if it will not put me into any jeopardy.

Maimuna: I wish I could stop gazing at you but I can't.

Ishaq: By the way, what's your name?

Maimuna: Maimuna.

Ishaq: Wow! Nice name, where do you live?

Maimuna: I live in Pakaliba.

Ishaq: You'd look strange to me and do not even look like a native of Dankunku.

Maimuna: Oh really? I have a special thing to discuss with you.

Ishaq: Go ahead—I only hope it won't take too long?

(A call is heard from the distance)

Ishaq: I have to go. See you some other time.

(Back to the occasion)

37

Imam Ratib: The winner for this year's competition is...Ishaq Ibn Saliman Bah!

Crowd: *(cheers)*.

Oustas: To give the closing remarks, I will like to once again felicitate all the participants, as well as those who were not able to make it. The winner is one of my students and while in my school, he was hard working, unruffled and time-conscious. He has memorized the whole Qur'an in just three days; a piece of soap does not wash itself and that's why I am saying this. It could have been anyone of you provided that you strove harder. This is what was left here for us by our forefathers and it is our duty to hand it down from one generation to another.

SCENE SEVEN

Awa is not the least happy that her son did not win the competition. She summons him and his sister, Oumie.

Awa: My children, I came to this earth before you. My eyes have seen what your eyes have not seen. My ears have heard what your ears have not heard, and I wish you take a walk in my shoe and see what I have been through. Since the death of your father, things have completely changed in our compound. Your eyes and ears must have told you this.

Oumie: Mother, sorry I don't mean to cut you short, but you are quite right. Besides, you are the first wife and therefore, you should do everything possible to correct the situation we are facing right now.

Awa: My daughter, you won't understand. Fatou and her children are fighting us by all means to corner the riches of your father to themselves. History has it that it is part of our tradition for me to even succeed your father on the throne. Was it not that that we have a matrilineal system of kingship, your father and I were sanctified by tradition in order for him to become a powerful ruler. But how come the Council of Elders could forget the link between culture and history?

Sheriff: Yes, even the Qur'anic competition was not fair. Everyone wanted Ishaq to win and so that's why he won. We have to do something about all these!

Awa: It will be a prolongation of what we have already started; you remember how I killed your half-twin brothers, Sainey and Sanna? I tell you this time that I must do everything possible to make Ishaq perish with his greedy mother.

Oumie: Mother, could you stop humming and pleading instead of treating? What's your plan?

Awa: Plan...just that I have considered visiting one great man in Janjanbureh.

Oumie: That's a total waste of time and money— you know you are to cook on Wednesdays and Thursdays. Why not you poison his food? You know what I mean.

Sheriff: Mother, Oumie is right. We must hurry up to stop the undulating stone from entering into the hole it is heading to. If he reaches twenty-four, he will be crowned by the Council of Elders as our king. As I am talking to you, that's what they have already decided.

Awa: What? May God shut your mouth with thunder and lightning for uttering such a word. A king? Over my dead body!

(Light converts and picks Ishaq where he is sitting, at an isolated place reciting Suratul Jinn. Maimuna appears to him)

SCENE EIGHT

Ishaq sits alone in a forest, holding his Qur'an on his right hand reciting Suratul Jinn. Maimuna, who will not let him sit alone, appears to him looking lovable and inexplicably beautiful; with pearls and golden jewelleries complementing her beauty. She shines brighter than fifteen-days-moonlight.

Maimuna: My dear, why do you like reciting Suratul Jinn all the time?

Ishaq: It's just my favourite Surah.

Maimuna: Well, today I bring you gifts.

Ishaq: Gifts? You must be joking!

Maimuna: Yes, gifts. Only two things, a bead and a pen.

(She gives the gifts to him)

Ishaq: Thank you dear, but can I ask you a question?

Maimuna: Yes you may, go ahead and hope is not about the gifts? Well, as for the pen you take it along with you anywhere you go to, and the bead you can use it to beseech the name of our Lord. They are symbols of authority, so please make the best use of them.

Ishaq: That's very kind of you. Ok, thank you once again and I will do as you say.

Maimuna: You must be very lucky, oh God! You are someone you don't even know but before I tell you anything again, can you tell me how old you are?

Ishaq: Well, I am twenty this year.

Maimuna: You must be joking! Meaning you have four years to be crowned a king!

Ishaq: A king! I hate leading and who told you that?

Maimuna: Leaders are chosen by God and not by people; for people can only recommend a leader by voting or nominating him or her. If He chooses you, why not you take it in a good faith?

Ishaq: One thing I don't still comprehend about you is that you keep on appearing and disappearing from me and you seem to be spiritually inclined. Can you tell me about yourself and family?

Maimuna: I am just a human being like you. Ishaq look, to be candid with you, I admire you. In other words, I am attracted to you.

Ishaq: Hey! I never knew that you shared veins with William Shakespeare! I don't understand your jargons!

Maimuna: Dear, stop pretending. I mean I love you.

Ishaq: How can you love someone you don't know? Do you know that I am the poorest of the poor, and have never been loved before? Why have you chosen to love me?

Maimuna: That's best known to God. We have certain qualities in common and I am to save you from all the bad elements of human race, among Jinns and demons.

Ishaq: You...you can't be serious! Okay, can you be frank and tell me who are you and what are you?

Maimuna: We have not come to that...I have to go but when your food is served to you on Wednesday and Thursday, please don't eat it. I will provide you food ok.

(Maimuna disappears)

SCENE NINE

Awa and her children are having a discussion about their failed plan to assassinate Ishaq.

Awa: Who must have told him our plan?

Sheriff: That's what I cannot just comprehend.

Astou: Mother, this is unthinkable, he barely escaped death...I wish he ate that food.

Sheriff: You have all done your part, now is left with mine. I will kill him with my hands while he is asleep.

Awa: Good idea! There are more ways of beating a bull than beefing him at once. If your plan hasn't worked, mine will surely work.

(Ishaq is so worried about Maimuna and also wants to know who she is, and the reason why she has chosen him. He decides to visit his Oustas and on his way, he meets Mariama)

SCENE TEN

Mariama, also a Jinn, has been listening to all the conversations Ishaq have been having with Maimuna. She too loves Ishaq and does not know how to tell him. She decided to make his journey long and appear to him on his way to see his Oustas.

Ishaq: Am I lost or what? This is not the way to my Ousta's home. But what brought me here? No, this is impossible. *Haaah*! No, let me take the other way.

(He sees the most beautiful woman the world has ever born, walking towards him)

Mariama: Ishaq Ibn Saliman Bah, what are you doing here by this time of the day?

(Before he could utter any word, he trembles and fall into a deep affection)

Ishaq: *'Wala-qad-karramna-baanii-Adaam'*. You— call...me by my...*hmm*...full name. You seem to know me very well.

50

Mariama: I am compelled to. I was at the Qur'anic Recitation and I wanted to congratulate you since that day, but I couldn't. Well congrats! Where are you going to?

Ishaq: Thanks. I...hmm...want to...see my Oustas, I...

Mariama: If you will not mind to give me time to discuss something with you. Be comfortable, are you alright?

Ishaq: Yes I am. You know I like shaking my hands when talking. I am not too much in a hurry. Go ahead please!

Mariama: Can you see a black ant walking on a black stone in the dark?

Ishaq: No, except God wills. But I like the ring in your hand.

Mariama: Oh really! I can give it to you if you wish, but on only one condition.

Ishaq: What is that condition?

Mariama: On the condition that you will marry me and will never break my heart.

Ishaq: But I...am...in love and I can't...

Mariama: I don't want to hear that. You are a man and can marry up to four wives. All I am asking you to do for me is to love me. This ring is not ordinary, and it makes you powerful, famous, intelligent and very wealthy. Are you afraid of me?

Ishaq: Afraid of you! Based on what reason?

Mariama: I am a Jinn and not a human being.

Ishaq: That is not a problem. Besides, I like Jinns. But you Jinns, when you get marry to us after seven years, you must leave us. I am not ready for that but if you can promise me that you will not leave me, then I am all yours because what you are asking me... I am about to refuse, but suddenly, my heart is already in love with you. I don't know whether I am under a spell or what.

Mariama: I promise I will never let you go. Here is the ring. It is our engagement ring and don't ever remove it from your hand and you must follow me to my fatherland. I must introduce you to my parents and hear from them.

(Ishaq puts the ring on his right hand and disappears with her)

After 10 minutes, he sees himself at the gate of his Oustas.

Ishaq: Ya-Mudirr, I am disconcerted by a Young Girl who keeps on changing her face from one person to another whenever I am in the midst of people. She gave me these pen and bead as gifts. She always tells me about God but whenever am with her, her face changes to be dark, wide and her eye-balls usually beam with light. She is fair in complexion and has dark eye lids.

Oustas: Oh my son, you have a great future. I don't know what some people like you did for God the Almighty to merit such a tangible reward on the face of the earth. I will tell you that anytime she comes to visit you, please take her to a place exposed to light and then recite *Ayal-tul-khursiyu*. You will see her reaction by yourself and can answer your question.

Ishaq: Oh thank you Ya-Oustas! I will do as you said.

SCENE ELEVEN

Sheriff attempted to kill Ishaq. As a matter-of-fact, that man was born envious and the more he envies the more evil he becomes. This makes some human beings to be so wicked than their fellows and must do anything possible to eliminate you. No one can ever stop a person from getting what God says he will get.

(Inside Ishaq's room, Sheriff enters surreptitiously)

Sheriff: Thank God he is sleeping. This is going to be his last sleep on the face of the earth, for if he doesn't want to rest in peace, he can rest in pieces.

(Maimuna appears immediately at the spot. She loves Ishaq and is always ready to protect him. As Sheriff makes an attempt to stab Ishaq, she wakes him up).

Ishaq: Sheriff!! No, impossible! Is this you? What are you doing with a knife in my room?

Sheriff: I...*hmm*...sorry, no...okay I wanted to harvest some yams.

Ishaq: What—? Get out before I eat your lungs and your heart, your explanation is meaningless!

(He bows down to his knees and prays to God)

I testify that there is no god but Allah, and Muhammed (S.A.W) is a true messenger of God. Almighty God I thank You. You are not an intolerant God and You are Merciful, the Beneficent, the Protector and the King of the Universe. I am only Your servant and in Your hands I shall return. Please protect me, whether I worship You or not. That will not benefit You anything. I live by Your mercy. Amen!

(Daybreak has come; Maimuna appears to Ishaq in his own room)

Maimuna: Good day, I don't like the ring in your hand?

Ishaq: Sh- sh!! Hope anyone did not see you?

Maimuna: No, not at all.

(He recalls what his Oustas told him. He switches-on the light quickly and recited the Ayah.)

Maimuna: Do you think I will be afraid?

Ishaq: Afraid of what?

Maimuna: Don't you know what you did?

Ishaq: Come on dear, don't let me waste time guessing!

Maimuna: You know what, I don't like what you did and please don't do it again. How could you do this to me? Where do you get this ring from?

Ishaq: Well—it's a gift from a friend. Please I just don't understand what you are saying; I can't kill an ant, so how could I hurt you? A man who really understands your tears will never make you cry.

Maimuna: A friend! You have never lied to me, don't take me for granted. To be candid, I cannot but tell you the truth. I am a Jinn, I am sorry that I didn't tell you earlier. I was afraid that you might leave me.

Ishaq: That's okay and I also truly love you. The important thing is not to stop questioning. But why telling me today?

Maimuna: I never had the courage to. I am afraid that you will reject me and I love you so much. Although I am a Jinn, but you have to know that both you and I are servants of God. I cannot force you to love me but I can tell you that you and I are meant to be together.

Ishaq: I don't hate you, but I have already…Sorry am talking too much. When the heart is willing the impossible becomes possible. Despite the fact that we are not the same doesn't matter in our relationship. I don't hate you, to be honest.

Maimuna: Then what's the opposite of hate?

Ishaq: Like.

Maimuna: No!! You are getting it all wrong, like and dislike, hate and love. Just be candid. Do you love me?

Ishaq: Yes I do and you alone I do love. I always ask God to show me my wife, whether she is a jinn, a human, a demon or whatever. All I need is someone who will love me for who I am, not what I have and, someone who will always understand my plight.

Maimuna: It is only when you are in love that you can see the eyes of love; I am not garrulous but I loved you since the first day I set my eyes on you. I cannot keep punishing myself for not telling you this.

Ishaq: Look that same day we met, I had prayed seven *Rakaats* to thank God the Almighty for knowing that by the time He was giving His beauty to women, you were the first person in the queue. Your beauty is beyond description.

Maimuna: Stop teasing me. In fact you are extremely funny.

Ishaq: You look like an angel, no sorry, like a fairy tale princess. What I like most about you is your candour and humility. Please forgive my eyes for admiring your beauty; but anytime my heart beats, it mentions your name. I wish I could die in your hands.

Maimuna: You can't be serious! You know, you men are like this. You always pamper us and make us adorable, but when you get what you want from us, you throw us into the dustbin of heartbreaks - like you never loved us before!

Ishaq: Now let us make it like this. I vow to you that I shall love only you and will never break your heart. I take you to be the mother of my children.

Maimuna: Don't you think you are making a mistake? Please remember that we are not the same. You are a human being and I am a Jinn.

Ishaq: I know that but I love you. Please forget about our individual differences and let the love we have for each other take its right reputable place in the family of reality.

Maimuna: Can you close your eyes dear?

Ishaq: No worries. Your wish is my command.

Maimuna: Look at me honey.

(She gives him a ring as well)

Ishaq: Wow! It's amazing, this is beautiful.

Maimuna: I have to go...but be warned that I don't like sharing my apple with another woman.

Ishaq: Ok but one thing, what are your likes and dislikes?

Maimuna: Smart boy! I hate lies, cheating, accusation, stealing, and dishonesty. I like somebody who is hard working, respectful, pious, intelligent, faithful, caring and kind.

Ishaq: Oh how is it that you speak my mind? Then we are compatible!

Maimuna: I will see you another time sweetheart, and goodbye.

(She disappears; light picked up Awa having a conversation with a Great Man in Pakaliba.)

SCENE THIRTEEN

The Great man having a discussion with the Jinn on Awa's plan to kill Ishaq

Jinn: Awa, the first wife of the late king, shall come to see you this afternoon. Make sure you watch your limits. Ishaq is the only asset this kingdom has and he must not die.

Great Man: Your orders will always dictate my consent. Just consider it done.

(A knock is heard at the door)

Great Man: Yes? You can enter. Awa Sowe-Bah you said you are a wife to the late King? What's that look on your face?

Awa: I am surprised that you call me by my full name! Have we met before?

Great Man: Ha-ha-ha. Go ahead tell me what you come here for.

Awa: A child wants to ruin my life for me. He is my step-son and stands as the only heir to the throne. Besides me as the first wife of the late

63

king, I think my son should be his successor. But to the contrary, my co-wife's son is the only person supported by the Council of Elders to be our next king. So I want him dead. This is my mission here.

Great Man: Well, as for that you have to pay me both in cash and kind.

Awa: Whatever! You just favour me and I promise to give you anything you desire.

Great Man: Good. Let's get inside and after I will give you all what you come here for.

(They enter the bedroom)

Awa: You made me feel young. Besides you have sufficient fire inside your gun. I promise that I shall make love again with you. I never had the chance to taste such pleasure and sweetness of a gun powder when my husband was alive. He was not mature enough in love but as for you, you are an expert.

Great Man: Take this bottle containing charm. You should sprinkle it in his room. As for the *juju*, you should tie it under his bed and the powder you spread it on the ground in the morning before he comes out of his house. In less than three days he is gone.

Awa: I will do exactly as you said.

Great Man: Make sure you don't forget to do it.

SCENE FOURTEEN

Ishaq is sick and he can not talk or open his eyes. In short, he is extremely sick and everybody is fretting, not knowing whether he will survive or not. He has been inflicted with a sickness by Mariama who is so jealous that he is in love with Maimuna at same time her. People love him so much, but who is to save his life?

Zaib: Great Cherno, what is it that has happened to our son?

Cherno: All is not well at all...the bee has stung herself in an attempt to kill the son of an ant, and unless she confesses both of them will be wingless.

Zaib: My ears have eaten hell, the worst has happened. Elders have you heard him?

Council of elders: Yes we do.

Cherno: Ah the gods have spoken...he needs to be saved by a young virgin or else, he will die. We have only three weeks to save his life.

Zaib: Elders, could we all at this juncture embark on a search for a young virgin?

(*They both scattered to search for a virgin in the kingdom. The days crawled, hours passed and minutes disappeared. They could not find one. Fortunately, Suaib saw one*)

Suaib: Young girl, all I am asking you to do for me and the entire kingdom is to protect the life of our Prince. Your reward shall be abundant. Our tradition has it that he must be saved by a virgin and it's hard to find one as you are. I can't tell you anything I have no knowledge of.

Young-Girl: A person is a person because of another person. I have no reason for denying someone my perfect body with the right goal of protecting his life.

Suaib: Then you must have to hurry up to get to the palace in time. We are left with only one hour to save his life.

(*They both rush to the Palace*).

SCENE FIFTEEN

One week later, the Council of Elders summon a meeting at the King's Palace to reward the Young-Girl who has protected Ishaq's life.

Zaib: I greet you all! We've called this meeting in order to reward the person to whom much should be given. As a result, we the Council of Elders have decided that we should give the Young-Girl's hand in marriage to our Prince for protecting his precious life.

(The meeting was thrown into chaos as Ishaq stood up on the dais to speak against the decision of the elders.)

Ishaq: Elders I greet you all...I must thank God first and the Young-Girl for saving my life.

(He discontinued and wanted to oppose the idea of getting married to the Young-Girl, but he thought of the respect he has for the Elders of the kingdom, having seen his Oustas and other important people, he acquiesced, bitter)

Light converted and picked Maimuna in an isolated place making a soliloquy.

SCENE SIXTEEN

Maimuna is soliloquising. She is so furious and disappointed with the decision of the Council of Elders

Maimuna: If only human beings would learn to treasure the simple pleasure of tranquillity, they will be transparent in their deeds. I am broken...only to know that Ishaq is about to get marry. I ask God why he didn't make me a human being. What have I done to deserve this? Where have I gone wrong so that I can correct my mistakes? If he mistakenly ties the knot with that girl, he will regret the day he was born.

(Mariama appears to her at the spot)

Mariama: There is nothing he will regret! Who the hell do you think you are?

Maimuna: You only speak when spoken to. Get out of my way.

(Maimuna tries to walk away and Mariama stopped her.)

Mariama: Let me warn you to stay away from my man before it's too late.

Maimuna: Your man! Did I hear you say your man? If not for the respect I have for your father, I would have burnt you into ashes.

Mariama: Conjure your spirits and let the war begin. I will show you the power I equally have.

Maimuna: Today you will know that all the lineage of Sowe Kunda, are born noble and deserves respect from the Bah Kunda.

(The duo evoke their spirits and fight each other bitterly)

In the end of the fight, Maimuna defeats Mariama; she surrenders and disappears permanently to live with the Jinns forever.

SCENE SEVENTEEN

Back to the Palace, the scene is in an open place where Ishaq was relaxing. Maimuna enters the palace.

Maimuna: Ishaq!!

Ishaq: Dear, you don't look exactly sorry about anything today. I want to talk to you. Can you help yourself with a seat?

Maimuna: I have not come to have any lengthy conversation with you. What do you want to tell me?

Ishaq: About my current predicament. Maimuna, I was forced to marry to a girl who saved my life. I wanted to refuse but couldn't. You must have heard about it. It is not fair to take away the pride of a woman and leave her like that.

Maimuna: Didn't I save your life? How could you be so heartless? You know I told you if you know you will one day break my heart, why not you leave me?

Ishaq: Did I say that I don't love you? You have to understand me and try to read the situation and put yourself in my position. If it were you what will you do? But at least you allow me marry her as well.

Maimuna: For your information, I am pregnant for you and won't let any man to use my poor body and dump me aside. I permit you to marry her but we will never live in the same house, and make sure she totally avoids you on Mondays, Thursdays and Fridays. If she doesn't, you will know my true colour.

(She disappears)

(Ishaq breaks into a soliloquy).

Ishaq: I have stepped on the tail of a sleeping lioness! Do I have to go forward or backwards? But what's the essence when the lioness has already been awoken. What should I do? Can somebody talk to me? Should I walk up to the Young Girl and tell her that I can't marry you when she already saved my life? No that's absolute madness! I have never heard of anyone married to jinn before! Aaahhh! I am talking too much. Do I forget the oath I took? But she said I can marry both of them... I wish the sky can change garments. To my dismay, I felt it so much when I took away the pride of the Young-Girl who saved my life. I had wanted to cry so much, it hurts that I nearly got drowned in my sweat. In fact, who do I love most among them? Well, I love Maimuna, but that lace is irresistibly beautiful. I was even thinking that she is a jinn as well. Really, God should be awarded the best creator and designer on earth. I only wish I can print him a certificate of honour because I'd know that it took him seven days to create that Young Girl. I will follow the dictates of my heart from now.

SCENE EIGHTEEN

The scene is in an open place where the Council of Elders assembled to discuss the marriage ceremony.

Cherno: Our elders of Niamina Dankunku, the gods are very anxious with you for making a choice for our Prince against his will. The success of our kingdom lies in the hands of a girl best known by our son himself, for if he fails to marry this girl, the whole kingdom will totally reduce to nothing.

Zaib: Great Cherno, we heard you right—and please forgive us for not consulting you. We did what we thought was best for the entire kingdom.

(The Young-Girl enters the crowd)

Young-Girl: If only a man should act beastly like a beast, I am sure he will be more beastly than the beast in the bush. How unfair on earth is it to take the pride of a woman and refuse to marry her? What a disheartening act is this?

Zaib: My daughter, the decisions of our gods are meant to be authoritative and none of us can put ice-block in their mouth. Don't be so neurotic. The merrier Marriage becomes, the more modest the many.

Cherno: The other thing is about the throne. Remember that it must not be left vacant for five years and this is now four years. We have to quickly make an effort to fill the vacancy. We must hurry to do this before the wind of affliction be blown from the grave of our ancestors. The gods have just informed me that our son can marry both of them. Salvation has arrived at long last.

(The elders later agree that they may marry each other to secure their throne.)

SCENE NINETEEN

(Ishaq is unhappy with himself and he sits at a quiet place and recites Suratul Jinn. Maimuna appears)

Maimuna: What do you need from me this time?

Ishaq: You and I have to talk seriously, because I want to fulfil the vow I have made to you. I swear without you my life itself is meaningless. I don't know whether you charmed me or not but my heart is married to your desires. You are the sight through which I must see the world, if you truly love me. You must also feel my sorrows not only my happiness.

Maimuna: Ishaq you are the land-lord of my heart, I always think of your happiness. You mean the world to me.

Ishaq: Maimuna I would do whatever it takes to make you happy.

Maimuna: You must follow me to my place where we shall stay for one year so that I can retain my human form, and after we can get marry.

Ishaq: Can I pack my things quickly? No, don't worry. I am alright like this. Let's go.

Maimuna: How could you be too hasty! Let's make it tomorrow. Very soon you will be happy, my sweetheart.

Ishaq: How soon is soon? Look I need you all by my side.

Maimuna: Darling, just wait till tomorrow, okay?

(She removes the golden-ring in her hand and puts it in Ishaq's hand, and they appear in the abode of the Jinns)

SCENE TWENTY

(Light fade away and picks the Council of Elders at the King's Palace.)

Zaib: Its one year now, we have searched for our son everywhere but cannot not find him. What is there that you suggest we do?

Elders: I think we have to pronounce Sheriff as our king because time waits for nobody and the throne must not be vacant.

Zaib: How can you forget so soon that we were instructed to make Ishaq the king and him alone as our Majesty?

Elders: We have no other choice than to secure the throne.

Zaib: Okay, your wish is always my command.

(The following day at the palace, it is the installation ceremony of the king.)

Sheriff: My elders, I greet you all! No matter how envious time is, it cannot deny the owner of success on a moonlight day. This kingdom shall be a relic of history under my leadership; I am certain of this fact because since I woke up this morning, I have not heard a voice of a crying child. This is symbolizing the commitment of my people towards me as a capable king and hope for change.

Awa: The upright establishes his throne through justice but the wicked greedy for power, and it is also said that if a king listens to lies all his servants become wicked. My son does not listen with his one ear, since the death of my husband.

(She pretends to cry)

We all know how dear he was to me and the legacy he has left for us. What is good for the goose is also good for the gander. What a man can do, another man can do better.

Fatou: Human is sense and evil is inhuman. A proposal which is written by God cannot be effaced by an eraser. If he has decided that Sheriff our son should be our king, why not we follow him? When the heart is sick, the whole body is affected, but when death is announced the evil becomes righteous. If you call your son a king, you will be the first person to pay tax to him.

Zaib: Enough! Let the ringworm reserve her brightness anytime the sun appears. God knows best our intention, but an intention cannot be hidden. I declare the meeting closed.

SCENE TWENTY-ONE

The late king appears to his son having been disturbed in his grave.

Ghost: Why don't you allow the sleeping dog to lie? You must hand over this crown to your brother.

Sheriff: Oh my God! Ghost! Here—ghost!!!!

Ghost: Hold it, you obstinate boy. A stubborn housefly follows the cadaver into the grave.

Sheriff: He is here! Someone help! Help! Please help!!!

(Cherno enters in the palace)

Cherno: The kingdom is reducing to doom, unless the right owner sits on it.

Sheriff gets into a frenzy, as Cherno warns him and takes his leave. The ghost disappears

SCENE TWENTY-TWO

The entire kingdom has converged at the King's Palace as people keep on dying, others blinded and many crippled.

I appeared to Astou inside the bush where she usually goes to in my temple to seek knowledge, I granted all her prayers. She was the last person seen to join the meeting.

Zaib: My people all is not well at all. As a result, we need someone to read the Holy Qur'an for us, from the beginning to the end, for us to quieten the spirit of our ancestor.

Crowd: They murmured—

Cherno: The only person who can do that has gone missing since nine months back.

Zaib: What can we do then?

Astou: My elders I greet you all! I must begin by telling you that there are four types of human beings on earth and they are: those who know and they don't talk; those who talk but they

92

don't know; those who know and talk and those who don't talk because they don't know.

Well it is left to you is to categorize yourselves into these four groups. Blood is thicker than water. If you know, you should share your wisdom with others. I can read the Holy Qur'an to save my people.

(The Kingdom's Praise singer starts praising her)

Gawlo: *Bah Pullo Jeerri*! A woman of decorum, house of wisdom and the tongue of the gods! She has spoken.

(Ishaq enters with Maimuna)

Crowd: Is this a ghost? Ghost!!!

Ishaq: If you think you must harm others to succeed, then you must also get ready to be wounded. Elders and my people I greet you all!

My step-mother and her children caused all this mayhem in our kingdom. I thought it should have been someone else but not the woman who has once slept at the back of my father.

The respect I gave her is inimitable, but a piece of cloth which should be worn on Tobaski day, if you wear it before the occasion for people to see it, anytime you wear it again it wouldn't be new to them.

Today they are all speechless and ashamed of what they have done to me and my mother and the entire kingdom at large.

(The Ghost enters in the crowd)

Crowd: *Murmured with fright and wanted to run.*

Ghost: My people—only those whom God have guided shall be guided, no matter how good or rich a dustbin is, it most eat garbage. A perfume cannot be stolen. Sheriff you must return the throne to Ishaq and let him marry Maimuna and the Young Girl.

(He disappeared, Awa died on the spot and Sheriff killed himself.)

(Some weeks later)

Light faded away and picked Suaib from where he was standing making a soliloquy and giving an epilogue).

Suaib: If only we human beings will learn to live and pay attention to the following things, then we shall live in a happy life: Wealth, Power, Love, Greed, Women, Satan and Children.

If we avoid taking the wrong direction in respect of the aforementioned roads, then peace will prevail forever on the face of the earth. There would be no wars, destructions, vendetta and all other crisis affecting humankind. A slave is powerless beneath his master, his master is also toothless under his master, people are powerless underneath their ruler, but all of them are slaves to God the Almighty. If you live in a glass house, do not throw stones and if you live in a hut, slum, mud-house or whatever, know that your time will come one day. Today is my wedding with Astou. Me a slave! Ha-ha-ha.

(Light faded out. The end of the play)

The End

Glossary

Assure - promise

Whirl - to cause something to spin round

Wean - to cause a baby or young animal to stop feeding from milk and eat only food

Aorta - the main artery which takes blood to the other parts of the body

Septum - the layer which divides the heart into two equal halves, the bottom of the heart

Lamentation - weeping

Soliloquy - a speech in a play which the character speaks to himself/herself or to people watching rather than the characters

Nimble- Footed- to be fast

Lad - a young boy or man

Providence - luck

Consecrated - blessed

Rivulet - a very small stream

Enshrined - encapsulated

Inalienable - unable to be taken

Realm - area of interest or activity

Vicinity - locality or area

Stammer - to speak or say something with unusual pauses or repeated sounds

Astounding - surprising

Jeopardy - danger

Engrave - carve or incise

Felicitate - congratulate

Unruffled - calm or tranquil

Allot - allocate

Prolongation - continuance

Perish - give up the ghost

Humming - whining or buzzing

Premeditated - planned or intended

Undulating - rolling

Affectionate - love or extol

Jargons - big words

Assassinate - kill

Unthinkable - ridiculous

Disconcerted - perturbed

Intolerant - bigoted or prejudice

Garrulous - a loquacious or talkative

Candour - frankness

Bounteousness - kindness

Virtuous - good or righteous

Successor - heir or descendant

Sprinkle - spray or spread

Fret – to be afraid

Dais - platform or podium

Virgin - someone who has never had sex
Neurotic - anxious or phobic
Pronounce - declare or name
Authoritative - respected or solid
Envy - jealous
Cadaver - corpse or death body
Temple - place of worshipping or holy place
Mitigate - alleviate or lessen
Decorum - good manners or modesty
Mayhem - havoc, chaos or confusion
Inimitable - unique, match or comparable

Glossary of Fulani and Arabic Words

1) *Bah Pullo Jeerri* it is use to praise the heroic deed of a Fulani tribe.

2) *Cow* meaning uncle in Fulani.

3) *Cherno* fortune teller in Fula language.

4) *Mi sallmi Nii oon bandirabeh* I greet you all Fulani

5) *Ya-Mudirr* an Islamic scholar

6) *Ya-Oustas* an Islamic or Quranic teacher

7) *Bakara to Naas* meaning from the first chapter to the last chapter of the holy Quran.

8) *Allahu laahilaha-illahuwa* a verse in Suratul Bakara.

9) *Suratul jinn* a surah in the holy Quran

10) *Bismillah* a verse in Suratul Fatiha.

11) *Janjanbureh* a town in the Gambia

12) *Pakaliba* a village in the Gambia

13) **_Niamina Dankunku_** a town in the Gambia.

14) **_Juju_** a protective charm made by the Marabouts.

15) **_Nimble footed_** meaning to be fast

16) **_Quranic_** having to do with the Quran.

17) **_Ayah_** *a phrase or verse from the Holy Quran*

Printed in the United States
By Bookmasters